About the Author

Mr. Sagar Salunke has 10 years of experience in automation testing including QTP(UFT) and Selenium Webdriver. He has worked on large investment banking projects in tier-1 Software Companies in India, USA and Switzerland.

He has designed automation frameworks in Selenium with Python that is widely used in the IT industry.

His hobbies include travelling, watching cricket and learning latest technological stuff.

A note of Thanks to My Wife

I would like to dedicate this book to my loving wife Priyanka for loving me so much and helping me write this book. Without her support, this book would not have been a reality.

Preface

These days lot of web applications are being developed to meet the growing demands of business.

So testing these applications is a big challenge. Automating test scenarios has become almost inevitable to reduce the overall cost and fast regression testing.

Selenium webdriver is the best open source testing framework that can be used to automate the testing activities in web application project.

In this book I have included all webdriver concepts with examples in Python.

For latest updates on selenium webdriver, you can visit my blog at below url.

http://www.selenium-interview-questions.blogspot.com

You can write to me at reply2sagar@gmail.com and you can join my facebook network at https://www.facebook.com/sagar.salunke.186

Table of Contents

1. SELENIUM Basics

1.1. What is Selenium?

Selenium is the open source web application testing framework released under apache license. Selenium can be installed on

1. Windows
2. Linux
3. Macintosh.

It supports programming in many languages as mentioned below.

1. Java
2. C#.Net
3. VB.Net
4. Python
5. Perl
6. PHP
7. Ruby

1.2. What is selenium webdriver?

Selenium WebDriver is the successor to Selenium RC. In earlier versions of selenium we needed Selenium RC server to execute the test scripts.

Now we can use webdriver to execute the test on particular browser. For each browser we have a separate web driver which accepts the selenium commands and drives the browser under test.

1.3. Browsers supported by Selenium.

Below is the list of browsers supported by the selenium webdriver.

1. Internet Explorer
2. Google Chrome
3. Firefox
4. Opera
5. Safari

Please note that for each browser, there is a separate web driver implementation.

1.4. Choosing technology for selenium.

As mentioned earlier, there are lot of languages that can be used for selenium scripting. Choosing the language depends upon the below factors.

1. Skill Set of employees in the organisation.
2. Training required on specific language.

I have selected Python as a programming language for selenium scripting. So in this book you will see all examples in Python only. But the same applies to other languages with some syntactical differences.

1.5. Installing selenium with Python.

Well – Now let us understand the installation steps for selenium in windows.

The list of Softwares you will need is given below.

1. Python Engine
2. Selenium Python API
3. Web driver for Chrome

You can download python msi from http://www.python.org/downloads and then install it. After installation, make sure that python command is accepted in the command prompt as shown below.

```
C:\Windows\system32\cmd.exe - python

Microsoft Windows [Version 6.1.7600]
Copyright (c) 2009 Microsoft Corporation.  All rights reserved.

C:\Users\sagar>python
Python 3.3.2 (v3.3.2:d047928ae3f6, May 16 2013, 00:03:43) [MSC v.1600 32 bit (In
tel)] on win32
Type "help", "copyright", "credits" or "license" for more information.
>>>
```

Figure 1 - python command

You will have to set the system variable Path as shown below. Please append the path to the existing value. In below figure I have included "D:\python33\" and "D:\python33\Scripts" in path variable.

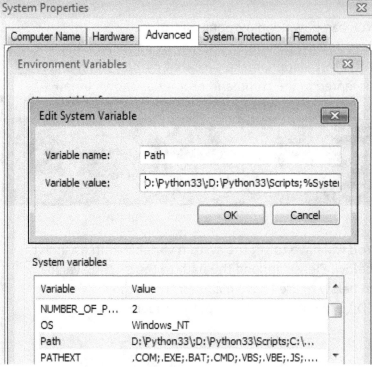

Figure 2 - Add the python path in PATH Variable

You can get the selenium API in python at
https://pypi.python.org/pypi/selenium Then you will have
to unzip it and then you will see below folder structure.

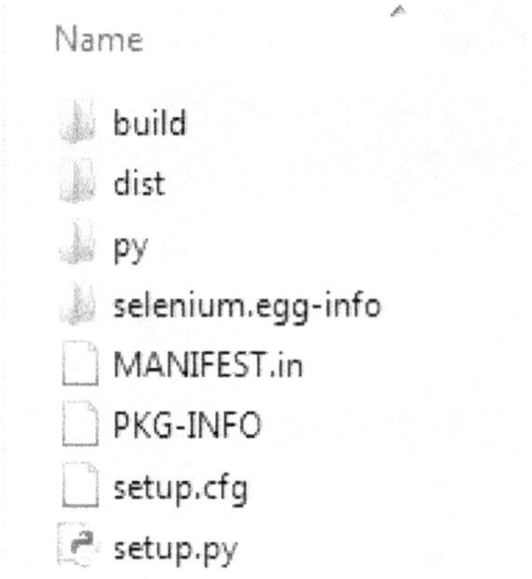

Name

build
dist
py
selenium.egg-info
MANIFEST.in
PKG-INFO
setup.cfg
setup.py

Figure 3 - Selenium Folder Structure

To install selenium package, you will need to run below command in command prompt

> python C:\Python33\selenium-2.39.0\setup.py install

You may get below error while installing the selenium package.
package directory py\selenium does not exist python

To fix above error you will have to Make Selenium (where you have unzipped the selenium package) your working directory and then execute the command.

1.6 IDE for Python

There are many IDEs available for python. I am going to use IDLE IDE that comes with python installer. PythonWin is anohter popular IDE.

You can launch it from (installation directory):\Python33\Lib\idlelib\idle.py

Once you have these softwares with you, You can follow below steps.

- Open python IDE from (installation directory):Python33\Lib\idlelib\idle.py .

- Go to file menu and then open new window

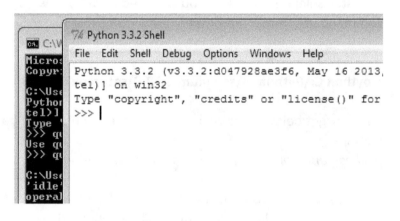

Figure 4 - Python IDLE Shell Window

```
74 f.py - D:\Python33\f.py
File  Edit  Format  Run  Options  Windows  Help

import os
from selenium import webdriver

#chromedriver = "D:\\Python33\\Scripts"
#os.environ["webdriver.chrome.driver"] = chromedriver

driver = webdriver.Firefox()
driver.get("http://register.rediff.com/register/register.php")
driver.quit()
```

Figure 5 – Window showing Python Program

2. First Script in Selenium Webdriver

Before I jump to first script in selenium webdriver, let me tell you how you can use developer tool provided by browsers like IE, chrome, firefox while automating the web applications.

<u>Inspecting Elements in Google Chrome.</u>

Google chrome provides very nice tool to inspect the elements on the webpage. You have to just right click on the web element and then select last menu item from the context menu – Inspect. After you click on it, You will see the source code of that element as displayed in below image.

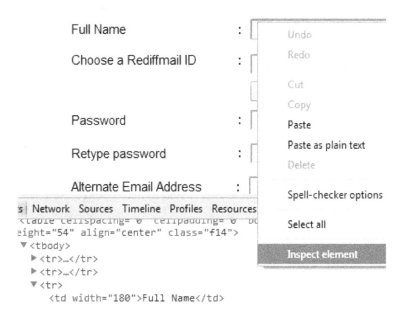

Figure 6 - Inspecting Elements in Chrome

Inspecting Elements in Internet Explorer.

Internet Explorer 10 and higher provides the developer tools from wehre you can inspect the elements on the webpage. You have to click on the arrow (circled in th red) and then click on the element on the webpage as displayed in below image.

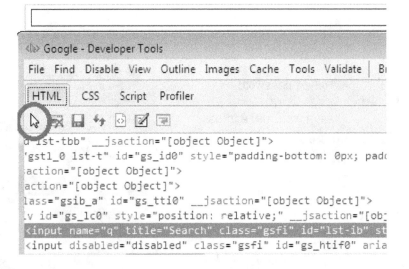

Figure 7 - Inspecting Elements in IE

Inspecting Elements in FireFox.

Inspecting elements in firefox is similar to chrome.
Inspecting elements will help you knowing the attributes
of the elements like name, id etc. which in turn can be
used in selenium scripts.

Figure 8 - Inspecting element in Firefox

Let us start with scripting right away. Have a look at below example.

2.1.Sample Program

```python
from selenium import webdriver
# Comments start with # symbol

driver = webdriver.Firefox()

#driver = webdriver.Chrome("D:\\chromedriver.exe")
#driver = webdriver.Chrome("D:\\iedriverserver.exe")

driver.get("http://register.rediff.com/register/register.php")

driver.quit()
```

2.2.Explaination

The *selenium.webdriver* module provides all the WebDriver implementations like Firefox, Chrome, Ie and Remote.

In above program, we have created the new instance of Web Driver for firefox. Then we have used get method to navigate to particular URL

Finally we have used quit method to close the browser.

3. How to identify elements in SELENIUM

As illustarted in the first program, It is very simple to create the webdriver instance and navigate to the webpage. In testing web application we need to perform operations on the webpage like clicking on the link or button, selecting the checkbox or radiobutton, choosing an item from the dropdown etc.

In selenium terminology, all objects in webpage are treated as webelements. So it is very important to identify the elements first and then perform some operations on them. Selenium provides plenty of methods to identify the web elements as mentioned below.

1. Xpath
2. CSS
3. Id
4. Name
5. Class Name
6. Tag Name
7. Link Text
8. Parial Link Text

We are going to look into each of these methods one by one.

3.1 Xpath

Xpath is the web technology/standard that is used to access elements from the webpage or xml document.

Detailed discussion of the xpath is beyond the scope of this book. We will see just simple examples to give you the idea of xpath. You can learn the basics of xpath at http://www.w3schools.com/xpath/xpath_syntax.asp

Examples – Suppose you want to identify the link of which href attribute contains google.

Xpath expression for above example -
//a[contains(@href,'google')]

Below code will find the web text box with id attribute equals to country.

```
element = driver.find_element_by_xpath("//input[@id='country']")
```

Below table gives some sample xpath expressions.

Find all elements with tag input	//input
Find all input tag element having attribute type = 'hidden'	//input[@type='hidden']
Find all input tag element having attribute type = 'hidden' and name attribute = 'ren'	//input[@type='hidden'][@name='ren']
Find all input tag element with attribute type containing 'hid'	//input[contains(@type,'hid')]
Find all input tag element with attribute type starting with 'hid'	//input[starts-with(@type,'hid')]
Find all elements having innertext = 'password'	//*[text()='Password']
Find all td elements having innertext = 'password'	//td[text()='Password']

Find all next siblings of td tag having innertext = 'gender'	`//td[text()='Gender']//follow ing-sibling::*`
Find all elements in the 2nd next sibling of td tag having innertext = 'gender'	`//td[text()='Gender']//follow ing-sibling::*[2]//*`
Find input elements in the 2nd next sibling of td tag having innertext = 'gender'	`//td[text()='Gender']//follow ing-sibling::*[2]//input`
Find the td which contains font element containing the text '12'	`//td[font[contains(text(),'12 ')]]`
Find all the preceding siblings of the td which contains font element containing the text '12'	`//td[font[contains(text(),'12 ')]]//preceding-sibling::*`

Below example illustrates how we can use xpath in selenium webdriver using Python.

```
from selenium import webdriver

#driver =
webdriver.Chrome("F:\\selenium\\Csh
arp\\iedriverserver.exe")

#driver =
webdriver.Chrome("F:\\selenium\\Csh
arp\\chromedriver.exe")

driver = webdriver.Firefox()
```

```
driver.get("http://register.rediff.
com/register/register.php")

try:


driver.find_element_by_xpath("//inp
ut[@value='Check
availability']").click()

    driver.close()

except Exception as e:

    print ("Exception occured",
format(e));

finally:

    driver.quit()

    print ("finally")
```

You can also use below tools to learn xpath
    1.XPath Checker
    2.Firebug.

In google chrome, you can copy the xpath of any element very easily. Below fig shows how we can do it.

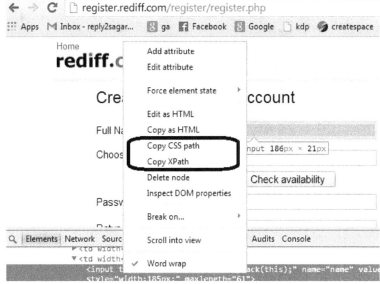

Figure 9 - Copy xpath and CSS path in Chrome

In other browsers like IE and FF also, you will find similar options in developer tools.

You can also use console window to try and test xpath and CSS expressions from the console window provided in chrome.

```
Q | Elements | Network  Sources  Timeline  Profiles  Resources  Audits  Console
       ▶<td width="14">…</td>
     ▼<td width="185">
         <input type="text" onblur="fieldTrack(this);" name="name" value
         style="width:185px;" maxlength="61">
       </td>
       <td width="6"></td>
     ▶<td width="272">…</td>
       </tr>
     ▶<tr> </tr>
 html  body  center  form  div#wrapper  table.f14  tbody  tr  td  input

 Console  Search  Emulation  Rendering
 ⃠  ▽   <top frame>                        ▼
 > $x("//input[@name='name']")
   [<input type="text" onblur="fieldTrack(this);" name="name" value style="width:185px;
 > $("input[name='name']");
   <input type="text" onblur="fieldTrack(this);" name="name" value style="width:185px;"
 > $$("input[name='name']");
   [<input type="text" onblur="fieldTrack(this);" name="name" value style="width:185px;
 >
```

Figure 10 - Console window in chrome

To test xpath expressions, you can use below syntax.
```
$x("//input[@name='name']")
```

To test CSS expressions, you can use below syntax. $ will return only first matched element.
```
$("input[name='name']")
```

To test CSS expressions, you can use below syntax. $$ will return all matched elements.
```
$$("input[name='name']")
```

3.2 CSS Selectors

CSS selectors can also be used to find the web elements in a web page. You can visit http://www.w3schools.com/cssref/css_selectors.asp to learn about css selectors.

```
we =
driver.find_element_by_css_selector("input[
@type='password']")
```

Above code will identify the first element having css selector as `input[@type='password']` and then click on it.

Below table shows commonly used css Selectors in Selenium.

Find all elements with tag input	`input`
Find all input tag element having attribute type = 'hidden'	`input[type='hidden']`
Find all input tag element having attribute type = 'hidden' and name attribute = 'ren'	`input[type='hidden'][name ='ren']`
Find all input tag element with attribute type containing 'hid'	`input[type*='hid']`
Find all input tag element with attribute type starting with 'hid'	`input[type^='hid']`
Find all input tag element with attribute type ending with 'den'	`input[type$='den']`

Below example demonstrates how we can use cssSelectors to identify the elements in Python.

```
from selenium import webdriver
```

```python
#driver =
webdriver.Chrome("F:\\selenium\\Csh
arp\\iedriverserver.exe")

#driver =
webdriver.Chrome("F:\\selenium\\Csh
arp\\chromedriver.exe")

driver = webdriver.Firefox()

driver.get("http://register.rediff.
com/register/register.php")

try:

driver.find_element_by_css_selector
("input[@type='password']").send_ke
ys("password")

driver.close()

except Exception as e:
    print ("Exception occured",
format(e));

finally:
    driver.quit()

    print ("finally")
```

3.3 Id

This method can be used to identify any object in the web page.

Only requirement is that the object should have a id attribute associated with it.

Example – Suppose you want to click on the button having id as "mobno". You can use below syntax to click on the button.

```
from selenium import webdriver

#driver =
webdriver.Chrome("F:\\selenium\\Csh
arp\\iedriverserver.exe")

#driver =
webdriver.Chrome("F:\\selenium\\Csh
arp\\chromedriver.exe")

driver = webdriver.Firefox()

driver.get("http://register.rediff.
com/register/register.php")

try:
    element =
driver.find_element_by_id("mobno")
    driver.close()

except Exception as e:

    print ("Exception occured",
format(e));

finally:
```

```
driver.quit()

print ("finally")
```

3.4 Name

This method can be used to identify any object in the web page.

Only requirement is that the object should have a name attribute associated with it.

Example – Suppose you want to find the edit box having element with name as – name, you can use below code.

```
from selenium import webdriver

#driver =
webdriver.Chrome("F:\\selenium\\Csh
arp\\iedriverserver.exe")

#driver =
webdriver.Chrome("F:\\selenium\\Csh
arp\\chromedriver.exe")


driver = webdriver.Firefox()

driver.get("http://register.rediff.
com/register/register.php")

try:

driver.find_element_by_name("name")
.send_keys("sagar")
```

```
driver.close()

except Exception as e:

    print ("Exception occured",
format(e));

finally:

    driver.quit()

    print ("finally")
```

3.5 Class Name

This method can be used to identify any object in the web page.
Only requirement is that the object should have a class attribute associated with it.
Example – Suppose you want to click on the button having class as "highlight". You can use below syntax to click on the button.

```
from selenium import webdriver

#driver =
webdriver.Chrome("F:\\selenium\\Csh
arp\\iedriverserver.exe")
```

```python
#driver =
webdriver.Chrome("F:\\selenium\\Csh
arp\\chromedriver.exe")

driver = webdriver.Firefox()

driver.get("http://register.rediff.
com/register/register.php")

try:
e =
driver.find_element_by_class_name("
highlight")

e.click()

driver.close()

except Exception as e:

    print ("Exception occured",
format(e));

finally:

    driver.quit()

    print ("finally")
```

3.6 Tag Name
This method can be used to identify any element in the web page with given tag.

Example – Suppose you want to click on the first link. You can use below code.

```python
from selenium import webdriver

#driver =
webdriver.Chrome("F:\\selenium\\Csh
arp\\iedriverserver.exe")

#driver =
webdriver.Chrome("F:\\selenium\\Csh
arp\\chromedriver.exe")

driver = webdriver.Firefox()

driver.get("http://register.rediff.
com/register/register.php")

try:

   firstinput =
element.find_elements_by_tag_name("
input")

   firstinput.send_keys("input-
data")

   driver.close()

except Exception as e:
```

```
    print ("Exception occured",
format(e));

finally:

    driver.quit()

    print ("finally")
```

3.7 LinkText

This method can be used to identify only links in the web page.

Example – Suppose you want to click on the link "Home". You can use below syntax to click on the link.

```
from selenium import webdriver

#driver =
webdriver.Chrome("F:\\selenium\\Csh
arp\\iedriverserver.exe")

#driver =
webdriver.Chrome("F:\\selenium\\Csh
arp\\chromedriver.exe")

driver = webdriver.Firefox()

driver.get("http://register.rediff.
com/register/register.php")

try:
```

```
  link =
driver.find_element_by_link_text("H
ome")

  link.click()

  driver.close()

except Exception as e:

    print ("Exception occured",
format(e));

finally:

    driver.quit()

    print ("finally")
```

3.8 Partial Link Text

This method can be used to identify only links in the web page.

Example – Suppose you want to click on the link with the text "google news". You can use below code.

```
from selenium import webdriver

#driver =
webdriver.Chrome("F:\\selenium\\Csh
arp\\iedriverserver.exe")
```

```python
#driver =
webdriver.Chrome("F:\\selenium\\Csh
arp\\chromedriver.exe")


driver = webdriver.Firefox()

driver.get("http://register.rediff.
com/register/register.php")

try:

  link =
driver.find_element_by_partial_link
_text("news")

  link.click()

  driver.close()

except Exception as e:

    print ("Exception occured",
format(e));

finally:

    driver.quit()

    print ("finally")
```

4. Performing User Actions in Selenium

Performing user actions involves identification of the elements on the webpage and then doing some operation like clicking on the button, entering the data in the editboxes, selecting a value from the drop down. Selenium Webdriver API in Python provides 3 important methods to enter data in web application.

1. send_keys
2. click
3. select_by_visible_text, select_by_index, select_by_value

4.1.Entering data in Editboxes

We can enter the data in the editboxes using sendkeys method as illustrated in the below example.

```python
from selenium import webdriver

#driver = webdriver.Chrome("F:\\selenium\\Csharp\\iedriverserver.exe")

#driver = webdriver.Chrome("F:\\selenium\\Csharp\\chromedriver.exe")

driver = webdriver.Firefox()

driver.get("http://register.rediff.com/register/register.php")
```

```python
try:

    driver.find_element_by_xpath("//inp
    ut[@name='name']").send_keys("Hello
    ")

    driver.close()

except Exception as e:

    print ("Exception occured",
    format(e));

finally:

    driver.quit()

    print ("finally")
```

4.2.Selecting a value from the Combo boxes.
We can select the value from the dropdown using 3 different methods.

1. **select_by_visible_text** – using the actual text displayed in drop down.
2. **select_by_value** –using the value of the option
3. **select_by_index** – using position of the item

Below example demonstrates how we can select the value from the drop down using `select_by_visible_text` method.

```python
from selenium import webdriver

from selenium.webdriver.support.ui
import Select

driver = webdriver.Firefox()

driver.get("http://register.rediff.
com/register/register.php")

driver.maximize_window()

try:

select=Select(driver.find_element_b
y_name('country'))

select.select_by_visible_text("Chin
a")

driver.close()

except Exception as e:

    print ("Exception occured",
format(e));

finally:
```

```
driver.quit()

print ("finally")
```

4.3.Clicking on buttons

We can click on the buttons using click method as illustrated in the below example.

```
from selenium import webdriver

from selenium.webdriver.support.ui
import Select


driver = webdriver.Firefox()

driver.maximize_window()

driver.get("http://www.amazon.in")

try:

driver.find_element_by_xpath("//*[@
id='twotabsearchtextbox']").send_ke
ys("Selenium")
```

```
driver.find_element_by_xpath("//*[@
id='nav-bar-inner']").click()

    driver.close()

except Exception as e:

    print ("Exception occured",
format(e));

finally:

    driver.quit()

    print ("finally")
```

4.4.Clicking on links

We can click on the links using click method as illustrated in the below example.

```
from selenium import webdriver

from selenium.webdriver.support.ui
import Select


driver = webdriver.Firefox()

driver.maximize_window()
```

```
driver.get ("http://www.amazon.in")

try:

    continue_link =
driver.find_element_by_link_text ('S
ell').click ()

    driver.close ()

except Exception as e:

    print ("Exception occured",
format (e));

finally:

    driver.quit ()

    print ("finally")
```

4.5.Setting on/off checkboxes

We can first see if the checkbox is selected using isselected method. Then using click method we can perform the operations such as selecting or deselecting the checkboxes as illustrated in the below example.

```
from selenium import webdriver
```

```python
from selenium.webdriver.support.ui
import Select


driver = webdriver.Firefox()

driver.maximize_window()

driver.get("http://register.rediff.
com/register/register.php")

try:

elem=
driver.find_element_by_name("chk_al
temail")

    if (elem.is_selected()):

        print("Checkbox is
selected..now deselecting")

        elem.click()

    else:

        print("Checkbox is not
selected..now selecting it")

        elem.click()

    driver.close()

except Exception as e:
```

```
    print ("Exception occured",
format(e));

finally:

    driver.quit()

    print ("finally")
```

4.6.Selecting the radiobutton

We can select the radiobutton using click method as illustrated in the below example.

```
from selenium import webdriver

from selenium.webdriver.support.ui
import Select


driver = webdriver.Firefox()

driver.maximize_window()

driver.get("http://register.rediff.
com/register/register.php")
```

```python
try:

driver.find_element_by_xpath("//*[@
id='wrapper']/table[2]/tbody/tr[21]
/td[3]/input[2]").click()

    driver.close()

except Exception as e:

    print ("Exception occured",
format(e));

finally:

    driver.quit()

    print ("finally")
```

5.Reading data from webpage in Selenium

Selenium API provides 2 important methods to read data from web elements.

1. **value_of_css_property** – gets the value of css property of the element
2. **get_attribute** – gets the value of given attribute.
3. **text** – gets the innertext of the element.

We can also check if

1. Element is displayed using **is_displayed** mehtod
2. Element is selected using **is_selected** method
3. Element is enabled using **is_enabled** method

```
x = e.value_of_css_property("width");

x = e.get_attribute("onfocus");


x = e.is_selected();

x = e.is_displayed();

x = e.isEnabled();
```

5.1.Reading data from Editboxes

We can get the data from editbox using 2 methods text and get_attribute methods as illustrated in the below example.

```
from selenium import webdriver
```

```python
driver = webdriver.Firefox()

driver.maximize_window()

driver.get("http://register.rediff.
com/register/register.php")

try:

driver.find_element_by_name("name")
.send_keys("sagar")

    elem=
driver.find_element_by_name("name")

    val=
elem.get_attribute('value')

    print(val)

    driver.close()

except Exception as e:

    print ("Exception occured",
format(e));

finally:

    driver.quit()

    print ("finally")
```

5.2.Reading data from combo boxes

We can get the data from combobox using 2 methods gettext and getattribute methods as illustrated in the below example.

```python
from selenium import webdriver

from selenium.webdriver.support.ui import Select


driver = webdriver.Firefox()

driver.maximize_window()

driver.get("http://register.rediff.com/register/register.php")

try:


 e = driver.find_element_by_name("DOB_Day")

 select = Select(e)

 select.select_by_index(3)

 selOption = select.first_selected_option
```

```python
print(selOption.get_attribute("valu
e"))

  driver.close()

except Exception as e:

    print ("Exception occured",
format(e));

finally:

    driver.quit()

    print ("finally")
```

5.3.Reading data from checkboxes

We can see if the checkbox is selected or not using is_selected as illustrated in the below example.

```python
from selenium import webdriver

from selenium.webdriver.support.ui
import Select

driver = webdriver.Firefox()

driver.maximize_window()
```

```python
driver.get("http://register.rediff.
com/register/register.php")

try:


    elem=
driver.find_element_by_name("chk_al
temail")
    #elem.click()

    if (elem.is_selected()):

        print("Checkbox is
selected")

    else:

        print("Checkbox is not
selected")

    driver.close()

except Exception as e:

    print ("Exception occured",
format(e));

finally:

    driver.quit()

    print ("finally")
```

5.4.Reading data from Radio Buttons

We can see if the radiobutton is selected or not using is_selected as illustrated in the below example.

```
from selenium import webdriver

from selenium.webdriver.support.ui
import Select

driver = webdriver.Firefox()

driver.maximize_window()

driver.get("http://register.rediff.
com/register/register.php")

try:

    elem=
driver.find_element_by_css_selector
("input[value='m']")

    #elem.click()

    if (elem.is_selected()):

        print("Radiobutton m is
selected")

    else:
```

```
        print("Radiobutton m is not
selected")

    driver.close()

except Exception as e:

    print ("Exception occured",
format(e));

finally:

    driver.quit()

    print ("finally")
```

5.5.Working with Tables in SELENIUM
Reading data from the table is very easy in selenium webdriver.

We can identify the table using name, Id or xpath and then we can access the rows one by one using findElements method.

For example – below statement will find all row elements from the given table. Please note that t stands for the table object you have found using findElement method.

```
tdcollection = t.find_elements_by_tag_name("td")
```

```
for td in tdcollection:
    print td.text
```

Another example – Below example illustrates how we can find the column number for the given column name in a table.

```
cells = t.find_elements_by_tag_name("th")
c = 0;

        for cell in cells:
            c=c+1;
            print(cell.text)
            if (columnName == cell.text):
                break
```

Another example – Below example illustrates how we can check if the value in given cell matches the desired value.

```
        mcells = r. find_elements_by_tag_name("td")

        c = 0
        flag = false

        for cell in mcells:
            c=c+1;
            if (c==a):
            {

#we can get the value inside cell using text property.

                if (expValue==cell.text):
                    flag = true;
            }

        }
```

6. Synchronization in SELENIUM

We can use below synchronization methods in selenium.

6.1 Page Load Synchrnoization – Implicit Wait

We can set the default page navigation timeout. Below statement will set the navigation timeout as 50. This means that selenium script will wait for maximum 50 seconds for page to load. If page does not load within 50 seconds, it will throw an exception.

driver.set_page_load_timeout(50)

6.2 Element Synchronization – Implicit Wait

We can set the default element existance timeout. Below statement will set the default object synchronization timeout as 20. This means that selenium script will wait for maximum 20 seconds for element to exist. If Web element does not exist within 20 seconds, it will throw an exception.

driver.implicitly_wait(20)

6.3 Synchronization based upon specific condition – Explicit Waits

We can also insert custom synchronization points in the script using WebDriverWait class. Please remember that you have to import this class before you use it.

```
from selenium.webdriver.support
import expected_conditions as EC
```

We can also instruct selenium to wait until element is in expected condition.

```python
from selenium.webdriver.support
import expected_conditions as EC

wait = WebDriverWait(driver, 10)

element =
wait.until(EC.element_to_be_clickab
le((By.ID,'someid')))


from selenium import webdriver

from selenium.webdriver.common.by
import By

from selenium.webdriver.support.ui
import WebDriverWait

# available since 2.4.0

from selenium.webdriver.support
import expected_conditions as EC

# available since 2.26.0

ff = webdriver.Firefox()

ff.get("http://somedomain/url_that_
delays_loading")
```

```python
try:

    element = WebDriverWait(ff,
10).until(EC.presence_of_element_lo
cated((By.ID, "myDynamicElement")))

finally:

    ff.quit()
```

7. Advanced Operations in Selenium

7.1 Mouse and keyboard Events in SELENIUM

With Selenium webdriver's Actions class, we can perform very complex keyboard and mouse operations.

Please note that we need to import below classes to perform below operations.

```
from selenium.webdriver import ActionChains
```

Using these methods, we can perform operations as mentioned below.

1. **Click (el)**
2. **click_and_hold**(el)
3. context_click(el)
4. double_click(el)
5. **drag_and_drop**(*source, target*)
6. **key_down**(*value, element=None*)
7. **key_up**(*value, element=None*)
8. **move_to_element**(*to_element*)
9. **perform**()
10. **release(key)**

Working with Actions class involves below steps.
1. Create Actions object
2. Generate sequence of action(s)
3. Get Action
4. Perform action

Examples -

<u>Below code will right click on the given element.</u>

```python
from selenium import webdriver

from selenium.webdriver.support.ui
import Select

from selenium.webdriver import
ActionChains

driver = webdriver.Firefox()

driver.maximize_window()

driver.set_page_load_timeout(50)

driver.implicitly_wait(20)

driver.get("http://register.rediff.
com/register/register.php")

try:

    elem=
driver.find_element_by_name("name")
    #elem.click()

#driver.save_screenshot("d:\\screen
shot.png")
```

```python
    action_chains =
ActionChains(driver)

action_chains.context_click(elem).p
erform()

    elem=
driver.find_element_by_css_selector
("input[value='eem']")

    if (elem.is_selected()):

        print("Radiobutton m is
selected")

    else:

        print("Radiobutton m is not
selected")

    driver.close()

except Exception as e:

    print ("Exception occured",
format(e));

finally:

    driver.quit()

    print ("finally")
```

Below code shows how we can drag and drop elements using selenium webdriver in Python.

```
from selenium.webdriver import
ActionChains


e1 =
driver.find_element_by_name("source
")

e2 =
driver.find_element_by_name("target
")

action_chains =
ActionChains(driver)

action_chains.drag_and_drop(e1, e2)
```

7.2. Taking Screen shots in SELENIUM

Below code will illustrate how we can take screen shots in selenium in Python.

```
from selenium import webdriver

from selenium.webdriver.support.ui
import Select

driver = webdriver.Firefox()

driver.maximize_window()
```

```python
driver.set_page_load_timeout(30)

driver.get("http://register.rediff.
com/register/register.php")

try:

    elem=
driver.find_element_by_css_selector
("input[value='m']")

    #take the scren shot

driver.save_screenshot("d:\\ishot.p
ng")

    if (elem.is_selected()):

        print("Radiobutton m is
selected")

    else:

        print("Radiobutton m is not
selected")

    driver.close()

except Exception as e:

    print ("Exception occured",
format(e));

finally:
```

```
driver.quit()

print ("finally")
```

7.3 Executing Java Script in SELENIUM

Below code will illustrate how we can execute java script in selenium in Python.

```
#Execute javascript in python
selenium

driver.execute_script("window.scrol
lTo(0,
document.body.scrollHeight);")
```

7.4 uploading files in SELENIUM

Uploading file using selenium webdriver is very simple. All you have to do is – find the input element having type attribute's value as file and then use sendKeys.

Below code will illustrate how we can upload a file using selenium webdriver in Python.

```
from selenium import webdriver

driver = webdriver.Firefox()

driver.maximize_window()
```

60

```
driver.get("http://register.rediff.
com/register/register.php")

try:

#here e is the file element


e=driver.find_element_by_name("uplo
ad")

    e.send_keys("c:\\abc.docx")
    e.submit()

    driver.close()

except Exception as e:

    print ("Exception occured",
format(e));

finally:

    driver.quit()

    print ("finally")
```

7.5 Downloading the files automatically

```
import os
```

```
from selenium import webdriver
    fp = webdriver.FirefoxProfile()

fp.set_preference("browser.download
.folderList",2)

fp.set_preference("browser.download
.manager.showWhenStarting",False)

fp.set_preference("browser.download
.dir", os.getcwd())

fp.set_preference("browser.helperAp
ps.neverAsk.saveToDisk",
"application/octet-stream")

    browser =
webdriver.Firefox(firefox_profile=f
p)

browser.get("http://pypi.python.org
/pypi/selenium")

browser.find_element_by_partial_lin
k_text("selenium-2").click()
```

7.6 Sending special keys

We can send special keys like Tab, Enter, F1, F2 etc using
below line of code

```
from selenium.webdriver.common.keys
import Keys

driver = webdriver.Firefox()

driver.get("http://www.python.org")

    elem =
driver.find_element_by_name("q")

    elem.send_keys("selenium")

    elem.send_keys(Keys.RETURN)
```

Other important keys are given below.
1. ALT
2. ARROW_DOWN (LEFT,RIGHT,UP)
3. BACKSPACE
4. CONTROL
5. DELETE
6. DOWN
7. END
8. F1 (F2, F3, F4)
9. HOME
10. TAB

7.7 Get current url , Title and Html Source

We can use below code to get the current url , title of the
web page and html source in Python selenium driver.

```python
from selenium import webdriver
from selenium.webdriver.support.ui
import Select
from selenium.webdriver import
ActionChains


driver = webdriver.Firefox()
driver.maximize_window()
driver.set_page_load_timeout(50)
driver.implicitly_wait(20)
driver.get("http://register.rediff.
com/register/register.php")

try:


    print (driver.current_url)
    print (driver.title)
    print (driver.page_source)

    driver.close()
except Exception as e:
    print ("Exception occured",
format(e))
finally:
    driver.quit()
    print ("finally")
```

8. Working with frames and Windows in SELENIUM

All web applications involve the frames, alerts and window. Selenium webdriver provides the way to handle with alerts, frames and windows using switchTo method

8.1 Handling Frames

To work with frames we need to switch to the frame and then perform the operation inside it.

We can identify the frame using 3 ways.

1. By index
2. By name
3. By using any of the identification method

Below code will switch to the 1st frame in the webpage.

```
driver.switch_to_frame(1)
```

Below code will switch to the frame with name xyz in the webpage.

```
driver.switch_to_frame("xyz")
```

Below code will switch to the frame with id f1 in the webpage.

```
e = driver.find_element_by_id("f1")
driver.switch_to_frame(e)
```

8.2 Working with Windows

Below code will show you how we can handle multiple browser windows in selenium in Python.

Python API provides one property called `current_window_handle` which returns the handle of the current browser window.

```
print (driver.current_window_handle)
```

When there are multiple browser windows we can access each of them using below line of code.

```
for handle in driver.window_handles:

    driver.switch_to_window(handle)

    print (handle)
```

8.2 Working with Alerts

We can handle alerts using Alert Interface in Python Web Driver.

At first, we need to get the alert reference using below syntax.

```
alert = driver.switch_to_alert()
```

Then we can click on Ok button using below syntax.

```
alert.accept()
```

Then we can click on Cancel button using below syntax.

```
alert.dismiss();
```

We can send keys to the alert using below method

```
alert.send_keys("kk")
```

To get the text displayed in the alert, you can use text property

```
alert.text
```

9. Important Built-in Function in Python.

9.1 Working with Strings in Python

We must know below string operations while working with selenium in python.

```
print ("Upper Case ->", "sagar
salunke ".upper())


print ("Capitalize -> ", "sagar
salunke ".capitalize())

print ("ends with  ->" , "sagar
salunke ".endswith("salunke" ))



print ("find sagar ->","sagar
salunke ".find("sagar"))

print ("Lower Case ->", "sagar
salunke ".lower())

print ("Stripped ->", "sagar
salunke ".strip())

print ("split ->", "sagar salunke
".split(" ")[1])
```

```python
print ("replaced ->", "sagar
salunke
".replace("sagar","ganesh"))

print ("len ->", len("sagar
salunke "))

print ("isdigit->", "sagar salunke
".isdigit())

print ("isalpha ->",
"sagarsalunke".isalpha())

print ("isnumeric ->",
u"123".isnumeric())

print ("isdecimal ->",
u"123".isdecimal())

print ("stripped site -> " ,
'www.example.com'.strip('cmowz.'))
```

Below is the output of the above python code

```
Upper Case -> SAGAR SALUNKE
Capitalize ->  Sagar salunke
ends with  -> False
find sagar -> 0
Lower Case -> sagar salunke
Stripped -> sagar salunke
split -> salunke
replaced -> ganesh salunke
len -> 14
isdigit-> False
isalpha -> True
```

```
isnumeric -> True
isdecimal -> True
stripped site ->  example
```

9.2 Working with Date and Time

In all banking projects, you will have to calculate the date differences or find the future or past date. So you must know how to do this in Python.

```python
import time;

from time import gmtime, strftime;

from datetime import datetime;

from datetime import timedelta;

#display current date and time

print ("time ", time.asctime(
time.localtime(time.time())))

#format the current date and time
print ("time", strftime("%Y-%m-%d
%H:%M:%S", gmtime()))

s = "August 16, 2012"
d = datetime.strptime(s, "%B %d,
%Y")

#add one day to given date
```

```
print (d +   timedelta(days=1))

#subtract one day from given date
print (d -   timedelta(days=1))
```

After you run above python code, you will get below output.

```
time  Thu Mar 13 10:01:48 2014
time 2014-03-13 04:31:48
2012-08-17 00:00:00
2012-08-15 00:00:00
```

9.3 Working with Files and Folders
Below code will create new file at given path and append some data in it. If file already exists, it will be overwritten.

```
try:
    fo = open("d:\\foo.txt", "a")

    fo.write( "Python is a great
language.\nYeah its great!!\n")

    # Close opend file

    fo.close()

    fh = open("d:\\foo.txt", "r")
```

```
    print(fh.read())

except IOError:

    print ("Error: can\'t find file
or read data")

except Exception as Ex:

    print ("Error: Exception occured
",  format(Ex))

else:
    print ("Written content in the
file successfully")
```

9.4 Maths

Important Maths related methods provided in Python are given below.

```
import math

#find the absolute value
print (math.fabs(-1)) #1.0

#find the ciel of number
print (math.ceil(1.89)) #2

#find the floor of the number
print (math.floor(1.89)) #1

#find the factorial of the number
```

```
print (math.factorial(4)) #24

#find the power of the given number
print (math.pow(4,2))#16.0

#find the square root of the number
print (math.sqrt(4)) #2.0

#round the number
print (round(4.6363,2))#4.64
```

10. Exception Handling in SELENIUM

We can handle the exceptions in python using try ..Except blocks just like try ..catch in Java

In below example , if any exception occurs in the try block, control goes to the exception blocks.

```python
try:
    fo = open("d:\\foo.txt", "a")

    fo.write( "Python is a great
language.\nYeah its great!!\n")

    # Close opend file

    fo.close()

    fh = open("d:\\foo.txt", "r")

    print(fh.read())

except IOError:

    print ("Error: can\'t find file
or read data")

except Exception as Ex:

    print ("Error: Exception occured
", format(Ex))
```

```
else:
    print ("Written content in the
file successfully")
```

In Selenium we have below kinds of exceptions that might occur in the code.

1. ElementNotSelectableException
2. ElementNotVisibleException
3. InvalidElementStateException
4. InvalidSelectorException
5. InvalidSwitchToTargetException
6. NoAlertPresentException
7. NoSuchAttributeException
8. MoveTargetOutOfBoundsException
9. NoSuchElementException
10. NoSuchFrameException
11. NoSuchWindowException
12. StaleElementReferenceException
13. UnexpectedTagNameException

11. Excel Programming in SELENIUM

Python packages - `xlsxwriter` and `xlrd` can be used to work with Microsoft excel workbooks. To install these packages you will have to download them in zip file from below urls

https://pypi.python.org/pypi/XlsxWriter

https://pypi.python.org/pypi/xlrd

You will have run below command to install both the packages.

> python setup.py install

Please note that you will have to run these commands from the respective directory of the package.

11.1 Creating and writing data to Excel Workbook

When we design a test automation framework in Selenium, we usually store the test data inside excel sheets.

Below example demonstrates how we can create and write to excel workbook.

```
import xlsxwriter

# Create an new Excel file and add
a worksheet.
```

```
workbook =
xlsxwriter.Workbook('d:\\python33\\
demo.xlsx')

worksheet =
workbook.add_worksheet()

# Widen the first column to make
the text clearer.
worksheet.set_column('A:A', 20)

# Add a bold format to use to
highlight cells.
bold = workbook.add_format({'bold':
True})

# Write some simple text.
worksheet.write('A1', 'Hello')

# Text with formatting.
worksheet.write('A2', 'World',
bold)

# Write some numbers, with
row/column notation.
worksheet.write(2, 0, 123)
worksheet.write(3, 0, 123.456)


workbook.close()
```

11.2 Reading data from existing workbook

We can read the data from excel sheets using below code.

```python
import xlrd

workbook =
xlrd.open_workbook('d:\\python33\\d
emo.xlsx')

worksheet =
workbook.sheet_by_name('Sheet1')

num_rows = worksheet.nrows - 1

num_cells = worksheet.ncols - 1

curr_row = -1


while curr_row < num_rows:

    curr_row += 1

    row = worksheet.row(curr_row)

    print ("Row:", curr_row)

    curr_cell = -1

    while curr_cell < num_cells:

        curr_cell += 1
```

```python
        # Cell Types: 0=Empty,
1=Text, 2=Number, 3=Date,
4=Boolean, 5=Error, 6=Blank

        cell_type =
worksheet.cell_type(curr_row,
curr_cell)

        cell_value =
worksheet.cell_value(curr_row,
curr_cell)

        print ('    ',
cell_type, ':', cell_value)
```

12. Framework Designing in SELENIUM

There are 3 types of automation frameworks that can be designed in selenium. Please note that In any other automation tools like QTP, Winrunner similar kinds of frameworks are popular.

Keyword Driven Framework :

In Keyword Driven Framework , Importance is given to functions than Test Data. when we have to test multiple functionality we can go for keyword frameworks. Each keyword is mapped to function in SELENIUM library and application.

DATA Driven Framework :

In data driven framework, importance is given to test data than multiple functionality of application. We design data driven framework to work with applications where we want to test same flow with different test data.

Hybrid Framework -

This is the combination of keyword and data driven frameworks.

After analyzing the application, you can decide what kind of framework best suits your needs and then you can design automation framework in SELENIUM.

Components of Keyword Driven framework

Keyword driven Automation Framework is most popular test automation framework. It is very easy to design and learn a keyword driven automation framework in SELENIUM.

In this article I will explain you all details about how we can design and use keyword driven automation framework in SELENIUM with example. I will also explain the advantages and disadvantages of keyword driven automation framework in SELENIUM.
In keyword driven automation framework, focus is mainly on kewords/functions and not the test data. This means we focus on creating the functions that are mapped to the functionality of the application.

For example - Suppose you have a flight reservation application which provides many features like

1. Login to the application

2. Search Flights

3. Book Flight tickets

4. Cancel Tickets

5. Fax Order

6. View Reports

To implement the keyword driven automation framework for this kind of application we will create functions in Python for each functionality mentioned above. We pass the test data and test object details to these functions.

The main components of keyword driven automation framework in SELENIUM

Each keyword driven automation framework has some common components as mentioned below.

1. Scripts Library

2. Test Data (generally in excel format)

3. SELENIUM - Settings and Environment Variables

4. Reports - (Generally in HTML format)

5. Test Driver Script Method

Test Data Sheet in keyword driven framework in SELENIUM.

Generally automated test cases are stored in excel sheets. From SELENIUM script ,we read excel file and then row by row we execute the functions in a test case. Each test case is implemented as a set of keywords.

Common columns in Data sheet are mentioned below.

1. Test case ID - Stores the Test Case ID mapped to Manual Test Cases.

2. Test Case Name - Name of the Test cases/ Scenario.

3. Execute Flag - if Marked Y -> Test case will be executed

4. Test_Step_Id - Steps in a test case

5. Keyword - Mapped to function in library file.

6. Object Types - Class of the object e.g winedit, webedit, swfbutton etc

7. Object Names -Names of objects in OR .

8. Object Values - Actual test data to be entered in the objects.

9. Parameter1 - This is used to control the execution flow in the function.

Test_ID	TC_Name	Execute	Test_Step_ID	Keyword	Object_Types	Object_Names	Object_Values	Parameter1
1	Login To App	Y	Step1	login	winedit;winedit	userid;password	salunke;mercury	
			Step2	Insert_Order	wincombobox;wincombobo	flyfrom;flyto	london;paris	
			Step3	Fax_Order				Order_Id

Please note that this is just a sample data sheet that can be used in keyword driven framework. There could be customized data sheets for each project depending upon the requirement and design.

For example there could be more parameters or test data is stored in the databases.

Test Driver Script in SELENIUM.

This is the heart of keyword driven / data driven frameworks. This is the main script that interacts with all modules mentioned above.

Main tasks that are accomplished by driver script are ->

1. Read data from the Environment variables.

2. Call report module to create Report folders / files

3. Read Excel file

4. Call the function mapped to keyword.

5. Log the result

www.ingramcontent.com/pod-product-compliance
Lightning Source LLC
Chambersburg PA
CBHW061020050326
40689CB00012B/2697